essential mediterranean

essential mediterranean

over 300 sun-drenched recipes

jacqueline clark and joanna farrow

HERMES HOUSE

This edition is published by Hermes House

Hermes House is an imprint of Anness Publishing Ltd
Hermes House, 88–89 Blackfriars Road, London SE1 8HA
tel. 020 7401 2077; fax 020 7633 9499; info@anness.com

A CIP catalogue record for this book is available from the British Library.

Publisher: Joanna Lorenz
Senior Cookery Editor: Linda Fraser
Editor: Emma Gray
Designer: Nigel Partridge
Proofreader: Richard McGinlay
Illustrator: Anna Koska

Previously published as *Healthy Mediterranean*

The majority of the recipes for this book were provided by Jacqueline Clark and Joanna Farrow; other
recipes were contributed by Angela Boggiano, Jacqueline Clark, Carole Clements, Roz Denny, Christine
France, Silvano Franco, Rebekah Hassan, Christine Ingram, Judy Jackson, Soheila Kimberley, Lesley
Mackley, Maggie Mayhew, Anne Sheasby, Steven Wheeler, Elizabeth Wolf-Cohen, Jeni Wright.

The majority of the photographs in this book were taken by Michelle Garrett, assisted by Dulce Ribiero;
other photographs were taken by William Adams-Lingwood, Karl Adamson, Edward Allwright, John
Heseltine, Amanda Heywood, Janine Hosegood, Patrick McLeavey.

1 3 5 7 9 10 8 6 4 2

NOTES

For all recipes, quantities are given in both metric and imperial measures and, where appropriate, measures are also
given in standard cups and spoons. Follow one set, but not a mixture, because they are not interchangeable.

Standard spoon and cup measures are level. 1 tsp = 5ml, 1 tbsp = 15ml, 1 cup = 250ml/8 fl oz

Australian standard tablespoons are 20ml. Australian readers should use 3 tsp in place of 1 tbsp for measuring small
quantities of gelatine, cornflour, salt etc.

Medium eggs should be used unless otherwise stated.

Contents

INTRODUCTION

When thinking of Mediterranean food, it is fresh, sun-ripened fruit, vegetables and herbs which immediately spring to mind. In the open-air markets, which are dotted throughout the region, stall holders pile high their fresh produce and offer it for sale. From Marseilles to Morocco and from Spain to Syria, wonderful arrays of salad leaves, garlic, tomatoes, courgettes, cherries, peaches, figs and aromatic herbs, such as basil and thyme, are temptingly displayed – the hot sun emphasizing the delicious flavours and pungent smells.

It should be no surprise to learn that the Mediterranean diet is a healthy one, since it is based on such fabulous fresh ingredients. Olive oil, which plays a major role in the cooking of the region, contains a high proportion of mono-unsaturated fats and research has proved its beneficial effect on health. The colour and flavour of olive oil varies in colour, from the golden Spanish varieties to the deep greens of some Greek, Provençal and Italian oils. Buy the best

extra virgin oil to use when the flavour is extra important, as when making salad dressings and mayonnaise-type sauces, such as aïoli and rouille, or for drizzling over roasted vegetables or stirring into pasta. When the oil is simply for sautéing onions or meat, a lighter, and less expensive, olive oil will be just as good, and, especially where the ingredients have more subtle flavours, will not overpower the dish.

The other staple ingredients of the countries surrounding the Mediterranean sea are bread and wine and these, along with olive oil, have been traded throughout the region for hundreds of years. With this trade came an exchange of produce and traditional recipes. Spices and aromatic flavourings were introduced through North Africa and the Arabic countries, and saffron, cloves, chillies, ginger and allspice are still popular all over the Mediterranean, appearing in both sweet and savoury dishes. Nuts, such as walnuts, almonds, pistachio nuts and pine nuts are also an ingredient common to many of the countries, and are used in all kinds of dishes, from soups and salads to breads, pastries and desserts.

Perhaps it is the sheer variety of cooking styles that makes Mediterranean cooking so exciting – and inviting. Vegetables, such as peppers, are sometimes sliced into thin sticks to serve as crudités with a flavourful dip, or tossed into a fresh leaf salad, but more often they are roasted to soften them and enhance their flavour, then combined with all manner of other ingredients. In Italy, tomatoes are sun-dried and tossed with tender artichoke hearts in a balsamic vinegar dressing to make a delicious antipasto dish, in Spain, fresh tomatoes and garlic are puréed to make a refreshing chilled soup, while in France, fennel, aubergines and garlic might be roasted around a flavourful corn-fed chicken to delicious effect.

The Mediterranean, of course, abounds with fish and seafood, and a visit to any local restaurant or taverna illustrates how unbeatable this fish, freshly caught and

LEFT: Glorious green-leafed marigolds shade juicy oranges in a grove near Seville.

simply cooked, can be: fresh hake cooked with olive oil, garlic and lots of parsley; prawns briefly grilled to accompany a hot chilli sauce; and mussels sautéed with garlic and herbs, or stirred into an exotic lobster stew. Meat, too, is prepared in simple flavourful ways; in Spain, lamb is often slow-cooked with red wine, garlic and peppers to make a hearty stew; or it can be formed into delicious meatballs and served Italian-style with melting mozzarella and strips of salty anchovies. Chicken is cooked in myriad ways, but most invitingly with tart lemon slices and lots of garlic to make a rich aromatic stew that in various guises is popular in several countries.

Bread is a staple food throughout the Mediterranean and always accompanies a meal, be it a bowl of soup or a platter of grilled fish. When you consider that it is made using the same basic ingredients, it is remarkable that there is such a variety of flavours and

ABOVE: A basket of ripe figs sit temptingly in the bright Mediterranean sunshine.

BELOW: Freshly cooked Greek bread flavoured with olives; simple but delicious fare.

textures. There are Italian soft breads, cooked simply with a topping of sea salt, or flavoured with sun-dried tomatoes and herbs, gorgeous Greek olive breads and delicious unleavened pitta breads, easy to buy ready-made, which are often used instead of knives and forks; when slit, the empty pocket makes a perfect container for salads, bean dishes and meats.

A peep in the display cabinets of any patisserie, confectioner or coffee house just about anywhere in the Mediterranean will reveal a feast of sweet treats. From highly decorated gâteaux to delicate cakes, biscuits and tarts, all Mediterranean sweets thrive on an abundance of fabulous flavours. Home-cooked desserts take full advantage of the glorious abundance of fresh fruits. For a special occasion, a colourful selection of seasonal fruits, such as peaches, apricots, melons and cherries make a stunning finale. Fresh fruits, such as figs, can be poached in a honey-sweetened syrup to serve with cream, and tart oranges can be turned into a refreshing sorbet and served French-style in the fruit shell. Dates are popular throughout the region: combined with an almond cream filling encased in crisp pastry, this medley of Mediterranean flavours makes a mouth-watering tart.

Mediterranean food is simple to cook, delicious and healthy. In this book, we have collected just a few of the vast repertoire of dishes from around the region, some traditional and others more contemporary, using classic ingredients, but creating something new – we hope that you enjoy cooking them and that we will bring a true Mediterranean flavour to your kitchen.

SOUPS AND STARTERS

*The weather doesn't have to be cold for soup to be appealing.
Across the Mediterranean there is a splendid array of soups
and starters to be enjoyed throughout the summer months, that
make the most of the abundance of fresh vegetables
and fruit available.*

ROASTED PEPPER ANTIPASTO

Jars of Italian mixed peppers in olive oil are now a common sight in many supermarkets. None, however, can compete with this colourful, freshly made version, perfect as a starter on its own, or with some Italian salamis and cold meats.

3 red peppers
2 yellow or orange peppers
2 green peppers
50g/2oz/½ cup sun-dried tomatoes in
oil, drained
1 garlic clove
30ml/2 tbsp balsamic vinegar
75ml/5 tbsp olive oil
few drops of chilli sauce
4 canned artichoke hearts, drained
and sliced
salt and ground black pepper
basil leaves, to garnish

SERVES 6

1 Preheat the oven to 200°C/ 400°F/Gas 6. Lightly oil a foil-lined baking sheet and place the whole peppers on the foil. Bake for about 45 minutes until beginning to char. Cover with a dish towel and leave to cool for 5 minutes.

2 Slice the sun-dried tomatoes into thin strips. Thinly slice the garlic. Set the tomatoes and garlic aside.

3 Beat together the vinegar, oil and chilli sauce, then season with a little salt and pepper.

4 Peel and slice the peppers. Mix with the artichokes, tomatoes and garlic. Pour over the dressing and scatter with the basil leaves.

FALAFEL

In North Africa these spicy fritters are made using dried broad beans, but chick-peas are much easier to buy. They are lovely served as a snack with garlicky yogurt or stuffed into warmed pitta bread.

150g/5oz/¾ cup dried chick-peas
1 large onion, roughly chopped
2 garlic cloves, roughly chopped
60ml/4 tbsp roughly chopped parsley
5ml/1 tsp cumin seeds, crushed
5ml/1 tsp coriander seeds, crushed
2.5ml/½ tsp baking powder
salt and ground black pepper
oil for deep frying
pitta bread, salad and yogurt, to serve

SERVES 4

1 Put the chick-peas in a bowl with plenty of cold water. Leave to soak overnight.

2 Drain the chick-peas and cover with water in a pan. Bring to the boil. Boil rapidly for 10 minutes. Reduce the heat and simmer for about 1 hour until soft. Drain.

3 Place in a food processor with the onion, garlic, parsley, cumin, coriander and baking powder. Add salt and pepper to taste. Process until the mixture forms a firm paste.

4 Shape the mixture into walnut-size balls and flatten them slightly. In a deep pan, heat 5cm/2in oil until a little of the mixture sizzles on the surface. Fry the falafel in batches until golden. Drain on kitchen paper and keep hot while frying the remainder. Serve warm in pitta bread, with salad and yogurt.

TAPENADE AND HERB AIOLI WITH SUMMER VEGETABLES

A beautiful platter of salad vegetables served with one or two interesting sauces makes a thoroughly appetizing and informal starter. This colourful French appetizer is perfect for entertaining as it can be prepared in advance.

FOR THE TAPENADE
175g/6oz/1½ cups pitted black olives
50g/2oz can anchovy fillets, drained
30ml/2 tbsp capers
120ml/4fl oz/½ cup olive oil
finely grated rind of 1 lemon
15ml/1 tbsp brandy (optional)
ground black pepper

FOR THE HERB AIOLI
2 egg yolks
5ml/1 tsp Dijon mustard
10ml/2 tsp white wine vinegar
250ml/8fl oz/1 cup light olive oil
45ml/3 tbsp chopped mixed fresh
herbs, such as chervil, parsley
or tarragon
30ml/2 tbsp chopped watercress
5 garlic cloves, crushed
salt and ground black pepper

TO SERVE
2 red peppers, seeded and cut into
wide strips
30ml/2 tbsp olive oil
225g/8oz new potatoes
115g/4oz green beans
225g/8oz baby carrots
225g/8oz young asparagus
12 quail's eggs (optional)
fresh herbs, to garnish
coarse salt for sprinkling

SERVES 6

1 To make the tapenade, finely chop the olives, anchovies and capers and beat together with the oil, lemon rind and brandy if using. (Alternatively, lightly process the ingredients in a blender or food processor, scraping down the mixture from the sides of the bowl if necessary.)

2 Season with pepper and blend in a little more oil if the mixture is very dry. Transfer to a serving dish.

3 To make the aïoli, beat together the egg yolks, mustard and vinegar. Gradually blend in the oil, a trickle at a time, whisking well after each addition until thick and smooth. Season with salt and pepper to taste, adding a little more vinegar if the aïoli tastes bland.

4 Stir in the mixed herbs, watercress and garlic, then transfer to a serving dish. Cover and put in the fridge.

5 Put the peppers on a foil-lined grill rack and brush with the oil. Grill under a high heat until just beginning to char.

6 Cook the potatoes in a large pan of boiling, salted water until just tender. Add the beans and carrots and cook for 1 minute. Add the asparagus and cook for a further 30 seconds. Drain the vegetables.

7 Cook the quail's eggs in boiling water for 2 minutes. Drain and remove half of each shell.

8 Arrange all the vegetables, eggs and sauces on a serving platter. Garnish with fresh herbs and serve with coarse salt for sprinkling.

COOK'S TIP
Keep any leftover sauces for serving with salads. The tapenade is also delicious tossed with pasta or spread on to warm toast.

GRILLED VEGETABLE TERRINE

A colourful, layered terrine, using all the vegetables associated with the Mediterranean.

2 large red peppers, quartered, cored and seeded
2 large yellow peppers, quartered, cored and seeded
1 large aubergine, sliced lengthways
2 large courgettes, sliced lengthways
90ml/6 tbsp olive oil
1 large red onion, thinly sliced
75g/3oz/½ cup raisins
15ml/1 tbsp tomato purée
15ml/1 tbsp red wine vinegar
400ml/14fl oz/1⅔ cups tomato juice
15g/½oz/2 tbsp powdered gelatine
fresh basil leaves, to garnish

FOR THE DRESSING
90ml/6 tbsp extra virgin olive oil
30ml/2 tbsp red wine vinegar
salt and ground black pepper

SERVES 6

1 Place the prepared red and yellow peppers skin side up under a hot grill and cook until the skins are blackened. Transfer to a bowl and cover with a plate. Leave to cool.

2 Arrange the aubergine and courgette slices on separate baking sheets. Brush them with a little oil and cook under the grill, turning occasionally, until tender and golden.

3 Heat the remaining olive oil in a frying pan, and add the sliced onion, raisins, tomato purée and red wine vinegar. Cook gently until soft and syrupy. Leave to cool in the frying pan.

4 Line a 1.75 litre/3 pint/7½ cup terrine with clear film, (it helps to lightly oil the terrine first) leaving a little hanging over the sides.

5 Pour half the tomato juice into a saucepan, and sprinkle with the gelatine. Dissolve gently over a low heat, stirring.

6 Place a layer of red peppers in the bottom of the terrine, and pour in enough of the tomato juice with gelatine to cover. Continue layering the aubergine, courgettes, yellow peppers and onion mixture, finishing with another layer of red peppers. Pour tomato juice over each layer of vegetables.

7 Add the remaining tomato juice to any left in the pan, and pour into the terrine. Give it a sharp tap, to disperse the juice. Cover the terrine and chill until set.

8 To make the dressing, whisk together the oil and vinegar, and season. Turn out the terrine and remove the clear film. Serve in thick slices, drizzled with dressing. Garnish with basil leaves.

CHILLED ALMOND SOUP

Unless you want to spend time pounding the ingredients for this dish by hand, a food processor is essential.
Then you'll find that this Spanish soup is very simple to make and refreshing to eat on a hot day.

115g/4oz fresh white bread
115g/4oz/1 cup blanched almonds
2 garlic cloves, sliced
75ml/5 tbsp olive oil
25ml/1½ tbsp sherry vinegar
salt and ground black pepper
toasted flaked almonds and
seedless green and black grapes,
halved and skinned, to garnish

SERVES 6

1 Break the bread into a bowl and pour over 150ml/¼ pint/⅔ cup cold water. Leave for 5 minutes.

2 Put the almonds and garlic in a blender or food processor and process until very finely ground. Blend in the soaked white bread.

3 Gradually add the oil until the mixture forms a smooth paste. Add the sherry vinegar then 600ml/1 pint/2½ cups cold water and process until smooth.

4 Transfer to a bowl and season with salt and pepper, adding a little more water if the soup is very thick. Chill for at least 2–3 hours.

5 Ladle the soup into bowls and scatter with the toasted almonds and skinned grapes.

GAZPACHO

There are many versions of this refreshingly chilled, pungent soup from southern Spain. All contain an
intense blend of tomatoes, peppers, cucumber and garlic; perfect on a hot summer's evening.

900g/2lb ripe tomatoes
1 cucumber
2 red peppers, seeded and
roughly chopped
2 garlic cloves, crushed
175g/6oz/3 cups fresh white
breadcrumbs
30ml/2 tbsp white wine vinegar
30ml/2 tbsp sun-dried tomato paste
90ml/6 tbsp olive oil
salt and ground black pepper

To finish
1 slice white bread, crust removed
and cut into cubes
30ml/2 tbsp olive oil
6–12 ice cubes
small bowl of mixed chopped
garnishes, such as tomato, cucumber,
red onion, hard-boiled egg and flat
leaf parsley or tarragon leaves

Serves 6

COOK'S TIP
The sun-dried tomato paste has been
added to accentuate the flavour of the
tomatoes. You might not need this if
you use a really flavoursome variety.

1 Plunge the tomatoes into
boiling water for 30 seconds,
then refresh in cold water. Peel away
the skins and quarter. Peel and
roughly chop the cucumber. Mix the
tomatoes and cucumber in a bowl
with the peppers, garlic, breadcrumbs, vinegar, tomato paste and
olive oil and season lightly with salt
and pepper.

2 Process half the mixture in a
blender or food processor until
fairly smooth. Process the remaining
mixture and mix with the first.

3 Check the seasoning and add a
little cold water if the soup is
too thick. Chill for several hours.

4 To finish, fry the bread in the
oil until golden. Spoon the soup
into bowls, adding one or two ice
cubes to each. Serve accompanied by
the croûtons and garnishes.

SEAFOOD SOUP WITH ROUILLE

This is a really chunky, aromatic mixed fish soup from France, flavoured with plenty of saffron and herbs. Rouille, a fiery hot paste, is served separately for everyone to swirl into their soup to flavour.

3 gurnard or red mullet, scaled
and gutted
12 large prawns
675g/1½ lb white fish, such as cod,
haddock, halibut or monkfish
225g/8oz fresh mussels
1 onion, quartered
5ml/1 tsp saffron strands
75ml/5 tbsp olive oil
1 fennel bulb, roughly chopped
4 garlic cloves, crushed
3 strips pared orange rind
4 thyme sprigs
675g/1½lb tomatoes or 400g/14oz can
chopped tomatoes
30ml/2 tbsp sun-dried tomato paste
3 bay leaves
salt and ground black pepper

FOR THE ROUILLE
1 red pepper, seeded and
roughly chopped
1 red chilli, seeded and sliced
2 garlic cloves, chopped
75ml/5 tbsp olive oil
15g/½oz/¼ cup fresh breadcrumbs

SERVES 6

2 Fillet the gurnard or mullet by cutting away the flesh from either side of the backbone, reserving the heads and bones. Cut the fillets into small chunks. Shell half the prawns and reserve the trimmings to make the stock. Skin the white fish, discarding any bones, and cut into large chunks. Scrub the mussels well, discarding any damaged ones or any open ones that do not close when tapped sharply with the back of a knife.

3 Put the fish trimmings and prawn trimmings in a saucepan with the onion and 1.2 litres/2 pints/5 cups water. Bring to the boil, then simmer gently for 30 minutes. Cool slightly and strain.

4 Soak the saffron in 15ml/1 tbsp boiling water. Heat 30ml/2 tbsp of the oil in a large sauté pan or saucepan. Add the gurnard or mullet and white fish and fry over a high heat for 1 minute. Drain.

1 To make the rouille, process the pepper, chilli, garlic, oil and breadcrumbs in a blender or food processor until smooth. Transfer to a serving dish and chill.

5 Heat the remaining oil and fry the fennel, garlic, orange rind and thyme until beginning to colour. Make up the strained stock to about 1.2 litres/2 pints/5 cups with water.

COOK'S TIP
To save time, order the fish and ask the fishmonger to fillet the gurnard or mullet for you.

6 If using fresh tomatoes, plunge them into boiling water for 30 seconds, then refresh in cold water. Peel and chop. Add the stock to the pan with the saffron, tomatoes, tomato paste and bay leaves. Season, bring almost to the boil, then simmer gently, covered, for 20 minutes.

7 Stir in the gurnard or mullet, white fish and prawns and add the mussels. Cover the pan and cook for 3–4 minutes. Discard any mussels that do not open. Serve the soup hot with the rouille.

PISTOU

A delicious vegetable soup from Nice in the south of France, served with a sun-dried tomato pesto, and fresh Parmesan cheese.

1 courgette, diced
1 small potato, diced
1 shallot, chopped
1 carrot, diced
225g/8oz can chopped tomatoes
1.2 litres/2 pints/5 cups vegetable stock
50g/2oz French beans, cut into
1cm/½in lengths
50g/2oz/½ cup frozen petits pois
50g/2oz/½ cup small pasta shapes
60–90ml/4–6 tbsp home-made or
bought pesto
15ml/1 tbsp sun-dried tomato paste
salt and ground black pepper
freshly grated Parmesan cheese,
to serve

SERVES 4–6

1 Place the courgette, potato, shallot, carrot and tomatoes in a large pan. Add the vegetable stock and season with salt and pepper. Bring to the boil, then cover and simmer for 20 minutes.

2 Add the French beans, petits pois and pasta. Cook for a further 10 minutes, until the pasta is tender. Adjust the seasoning.

3 Ladle the soup into individual bowls. Mix together the pesto and sun-dried tomato paste, and stir a spoonful into each serving. Serve with grated Parmesan cheese to sprinkle into each bowl.

CHILLED TOMATO AND SWEET PEPPER SOUP

A recipe inspired by the Spanish gazpacho, the difference being that this soup is cooked first, and then chilled.

2 red peppers, halved, cored
and seeded
45ml/3 tbsp olive oil
1 onion, finely chopped
2 garlic cloves, crushed
675g/1½ lb ripe well-flavoured
tomatoes
150ml/¼ pint/⅔ cup red wine
600ml/1 pint/2½ cups chicken stock
salt and ground black pepper
snipped fresh chives, to garnish

FOR THE CROUTONS
2 slices white bread, crusts removed
60ml/4 tbsp olive oil

SERVES 4

1 Cut each pepper half into quarters. Place skin side up on a grill rack and cook until the skins have charred. Transfer to a bowl and cover with a plate.

2 Heat the oil in a large pan. Add the onion and garlic and cook until soft. Meanwhile, remove the skin from the peppers and roughly chop them. Cut the tomatoes into chunks.

3 Add the peppers and tomatoes to the pan, then cover and cook gently for 10 minutes. Add the wine and cook for a further 5 minutes, then add the stock and salt and pepper and continue to simmer for 20 minutes.

4 To make the croûtons, cut the bread into cubes. Heat the oil in a small frying pan, add the bread and fry until golden. Drain on kitchen paper and store in an airtight box.

5 Process the soup in a blender or food processor until smooth. Pour into a clean glass or ceramic bowl and leave to cool thoroughly before chilling in the fridge for at least 3 hours. When the soup is cold, season to taste.

6 Serve the soup in bowls, topped with the croûtons and garnished with snipped chives.

RIBOLLITA

Ribollita is rather like minestrone, but includes beans instead of pasta. In Italy it is traditionally served ladled over bread and a rich green vegetable, although you could omit this for a lighter version.

45ml/3 tbsp olive oil
2 onions, chopped
2 carrots, sliced
4 garlic cloves, crushed
2 celery sticks, thinly sliced
1 fennel bulb, trimmed and chopped
2 large courgettes, thinly sliced
400g/14oz can chopped tomatoes
30ml/2 tbsp home-made or
bought pesto
900ml/1½ pints/3¾ cups vegetable
stock
400g/14oz can haricot or borlotti
beans, drained
salt and ground black pepper

To Finish
450g/1lb young spinach
15ml/1 tbsp extra virgin olive oil, plus
extra for drizzling
6–8 slices white bread
Parmesan cheese shavings

Serves 6–8

VARIATION
Use other dark greens, such as chard or cabbage instead of the spinach; shred and cook until tender.

 Heat the oil in a large saucepan. Add the onions, carrots, garlic, celery and fennel and fry gently for 10 minutes. Add the courgettes and fry for a further 2 minutes.

2 Add the chopped tomatoes, pesto, stock and beans and bring to the boil. Reduce the heat, cover and simmer gently for 25–30 minutes, until the vegetables are completely tender. Season with salt and pepper to taste.

3 To serve, fry the spinach in the oil for 2 minutes or until wilted. Spoon over the bread in soup bowls, then ladle the soup over the spinach. Serve with extra olive oil for drizzling on to the soup and Parmesan cheese to sprinkle on top.

SPANISH GARLIC SOUP

This is a simple and satisfying soup, made with one of the most popular ingredients in the Mediterranean — garlic!

30ml/2 tbsp olive oil
4 large garlic cloves, peeled
4 slices French bread, 5mm/¼in thick
15ml/1 tbsp paprika
1 litre/1¾ pints/4 cups beef stock
1.5ml/¼ tsp ground cumin
pinch of saffron strands
4 eggs
salt and ground black pepper
chopped fresh parsley, to garnish

SERVES 4

1 Preheat the oven to 230°C/ 450°F/Gas 8. Heat the oil in a large pan. Add the whole garlic cloves and cook until golden. Remove and set aside. Fry the bread in the oil until golden, then set aside.

2 Add the paprika to the pan, and fry for a few seconds. Stir in the beef stock, cumin and saffron, then add the reserved garlic, crushing the cloves with the back of a wooden spoon. Season with salt and pepper then cook for about 5 minutes.

3 Ladle the soup into four ovenproof bowls and break an egg into each. Place the slices of fried bread on top of the egg and place in the oven for about 3–4 minutes, until the eggs are set. Sprinkle with parsley and serve at once.

Vegetables and Vegetarian Dishes

Vegetables take pride of place on the Mediterranean table; with such a treasure trove of vegetables ranging from the exotic aubergine to the humble potato this is no wonder.

GRILLED AUBERGINE PARCELS

These are delicious little Italian bundles of tomatoes, mozzarella cheese and basil, wrapped in slices of aubergine.

2 large, long aubergines
225g/8oz mozzarella cheese
2 plum tomatoes
16 large basil leaves
salt and ground black pepper
30ml/2 tbsp olive oil

FOR THE DRESSING
60ml/4 tbsp olive oil
5ml/1 tsp balsamic vinegar
15ml/1 tbsp sun-dried tomato paste
15ml/1 tbsp lemon juice

FOR THE GARNISH
30ml/2 tbsp toasted pine nuts
torn basil leaves

SERVES 4

 Remove the stalks from the aubergines and cut the aubergines lengthways into thin slices – the aim is to get 16 slices in total, disregarding the first and last slices (each about 5mm/¼in thick). (If you have a mandolin, it will cut perfect, even slices for you, otherwise, use a long-bladed, sharp knife.)

 Bring a large pan of salted water to the boil and cook the aubergine slices for about 2 minutes, until just softened. Drain the sliced aubergines, then dry on kitchen paper.

 Cut the mozzarella cheese into eight slices. Cut each tomato into eight slices, not counting the first and last slices.

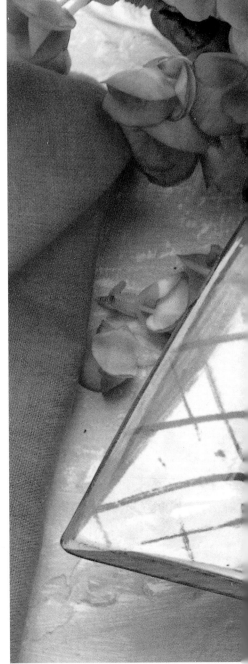

 Take two aubergine slices and place on a flameproof tray or dish, in a cross (*left*). Place a slice of tomato in the centre, season with salt and pepper, then add a basil leaf, followed by a slice of mozzarella, another basil leaf, a slice of tomato and more seasoning.

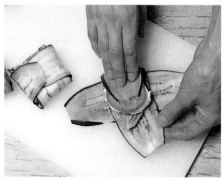

5 Fold the ends of the aubergine slices around the mozzarella and tomato filling to make a neat parcel (*left*). Repeat with the rest of the assembled ingredients to make eight parcels. Chill the parcels for about 20 minutes.

6 To make the tomato dressing, whisk together the olive oil, vinegar, sun-dried tomato paste and lemon juice. Season to taste.

7 Preheat the grill. Brush the parcels with olive oil and cook for about 5 minutes on each side, until golden. Serve hot, with the dressing, sprinkled with pine nuts and basil.

POLPETTES

Delicious little fried morsels of potato and Greek feta cheese, flavoured with dill and lemon juice.

500g/1¼lb potatoes
115g/4oz feta cheese
4 spring onions, chopped
45ml/3 tbsp chopped fresh dill
1 egg, beaten
15ml/1 tbsp lemon juice
salt and ground black pepper
flour for dredging
45ml/3 tbsp olive oil

SERVES 4

1. Boil the potatoes in their skins in lightly salted water until soft. Drain, then peel while still warm. Place in a bowl and mash. Crumble the feta cheese into the potatoes and add the spring onions, dill, egg and lemon juice and season with salt and pepper. (The cheese is salty, so taste before you add salt.) Stir well.

2. Cover the mixture and chill until firm. Divide the mixture into walnut-size balls, then flatten them slightly. Dredge with flour. Heat the oil in a frying pan and fry the polpettes until golden brown on each side. Drain on kitchen paper and serve at once.

SPINACH AND RICOTTA GNOCCHI

The success of this Italian dish lies in not overworking the mixture, to achieve delicious, light mouthfuls.

900g/2lb fresh spinach
350g/12oz/1½ cups ricotta cheese
60ml/4 tbsp freshly grated
Parmesan cheese
3 size 2 eggs, beaten
1.5ml/¼ tsp grated nutmeg
45–60ml/3– 4 tbsp plain flour
115g/4oz/½ cup butter, melted
salt and ground black pepper
freshly grated Parmesan cheese,
to serve

SERVES 4

1 Place the spinach in a large pan and cook for 5 minutes, until wilted. Leave to cool, then squeeze the spinach as dry as possible. Process in a blender or food processor, then transfer to a bowl.

2 Add the ricotta, Parmesan, eggs and nutmeg. Season with salt and pepper and mix together. Add enough flour to make the mixture into a soft dough. Using your hands, shape the mixture into 7.5cm/3in sausages, then dust lightly with flour.

3 Bring a large pan of salted water to the boil. Gently slide the gnocchi into the water and cook for 1–2 minutes, until they float to the surface. Remove the gnocchi with a slotted spoon and transfer to a warmed dish. Pour over the melted butter and sprinkle with Parmesan cheese. Serve at once.

STUFFED TOMATOES AND PEPPERS

Colourful peppers and tomatoes make perfect containers for various meat and vegetable stuffings. This rice and herb version uses typically Greek ingredients.

VARIATION

Small aubergines or large courgettes also make good vegetables for stuffing. Halve and scoop out the centres of the vegetables, then oil the vegetable cases and bake for about 15 minutes. Chop the centres, fry for 2–3 minutes to soften and add to the stuffing mixture. Fill the aubergine or courgette cases with the stuffing and bake as for the peppers and tomatoes.

2 large ripe tomatoes
1 green pepper
1 yellow or orange pepper
60ml/4 tbsp olive oil, plus extra
for sprinkling
2 onions, chopped
2 garlic cloves, crushed
50g/2oz/½ cup blanched
almonds, chopped
75g/3oz/scant ½ cup long grain rice,
boiled and drained
15g/½oz mint, roughly chopped
15g/½oz parsley, roughly chopped
25g/1oz/2 tbsp sultanas
45ml/3 tbsp ground almonds
salt and ground black pepper
chopped mixed herbs, to garnish

SERVES 4

1 Preheat the oven to 190°C/ 375°F/Gas 5. Cut the tomatoes in half and scoop out the pulp and seeds using a teaspoon. Leave the tomatoes to drain on kitchen paper with cut sides down. Roughly chop the tomato pulp and seeds.

2 Halve the peppers, leaving the cores intact. Scoop out the seeds. Brush the peppers with 15ml/ 1 tbsp of the oil and bake on a baking tray for 15 minutes. Place the peppers and tomatoes in a shallow ovenproof dish and season with salt and pepper.

3 Fry the onions in the remaining oil for 5 minutes. Add the garlic and chopped almonds and fry for a further minute.

4 Remove the pan from the heat and stir in the rice, chopped tomatoes, mint, parsley and sultanas. Season well with salt and pepper and spoon the mixture into the tomatoes and peppers.

5 Pour 150ml/¼ pint/⅔ cup boiling water around the tomatoes and peppers and bake, uncovered, for 20 minutes. Scatter with the ground almonds and sprinkle with a little extra olive oil. Return to the oven and bake for a further 20 minutes, or until turning golden. Serve garnished with fresh herbs.

COURGETTE FRITTERS WITH PISTOU

These delicious fritters are a speciality of Southern France. The pistou sauce provides a lovely contrast in flavour, but you could substitute other sauces, like a garlicky tomato one or a herb dressing.

FOR THE PISTOU
15g/½oz basil leaves
4 garlic cloves, crushed
90g/3½oz/1 cup grated
Parmesan cheese
finely grated rind of 1 lemon
150ml/¼ pint/⅔ cup olive oil

FOR THE FRITTERS
450g/1lb courgettes, grated
75g/3oz/⅔ cup plain flour
1 egg, separated
15ml/1 tbsp olive oil
oil for shallow frying
salt and ground black pepper

SERVES 4

1 To make the pistou, crush the basil leaves and garlic with a pestle and mortar to make a fairly fine paste. Transfer the paste to a bowl and stir in the grated cheese and lemon rind. Gradually blend in the oil, a little at a time, until combined, then transfer to a small serving dish.

2 To make the fritters, put the grated courgettes in a sieve over a bowl and sprinkle with plenty of salt. Leave for 1 hour then rinse thoroughly. Dry well on kitchen paper.

3 Sift the flour into a bowl and make a well in the centre, then add the egg yolk and oil. Measure 75ml/5 tbsp water and add a little to the bowl.

4 Whisk the egg yolk and oil, gradually incorporating the flour and water to make a smooth batter. Season and leave for 30 minutes.

5 Stir the courgettes into the batter. Whisk the egg white until stiff, then fold into the batter.

6 Heat 1cm/½in of oil in a frying pan. Add dessertspoons of batter to the oil and fry for 2 minutes until golden. Drain the fritters on kitchen paper and keep warm while frying the rest. Serve with the sauce.

RATATOUILLE

A highly versatile vegetable stew from Provence. Ratatouille is delicious hot or cold, on its own or with eggs, pasta, fish or meat – particularly roast lamb.

900g/2lb ripe, well-flavoured tomatoes
120ml/4fl oz/½ cup olive oil
2 onions, thinly sliced
2 red peppers, seeded and cut
into chunks
1 yellow or orange pepper, seeded and
cut into chunks
1 large aubergine, cut into chunks
2 courgettes, cut into thick slices
4 garlic cloves, crushed
2 bay leaves
15ml/1 tbsp chopped young thyme
salt and ground black pepper

SERVES 6

 Plunge the tomatoes into boiling water for 30 seconds, then refresh in cold water. Peel away the skins and chop roughly.

2 Heat a little of the oil in a large, heavy-based pan and fry the onions for 5 minutes. Add the peppers and fry for a further 2 minutes. Drain. Add the aubergines and more oil and fry gently for 5 minutes. Add the remaining oil and courgettes and fry for 3 minutes. Drain.

3 Add the garlic and tomatoes to the pan with the bay leaves and thyme and a little salt and pepper. Cook gently until the tomatoes have softened and are turning pulpy.

 Return all the vegetables to the pan and cook gently, stirring frequently, for about 15 minutes, until fairly pulpy but retaining a little texture. Season with more salt and pepper to taste.

COOK'S TIP
There are no specific quantities for the vegetables when making ratatouille so you can, to a large extent, vary the quantities and types of vegetables depending on what you have in the fridge. If the tomatoes are a little tasteless, add 30–45ml/2–3 tbsp tomato purée and a dash of sugar to the mixture along with the tomatoes.

SPINACH WITH RAISINS AND PINE NUTS

Raisins and pine nuts are frequent partners in Spanish recipes. Here, tossed with wilted spinach and croûtons, they make a delicious snack or main meal accompaniment.

50g/2oz/⅓ cup raisins
1 thick slice crusty white bread
45ml/3 tbsp olive oil
25g/1oz/⅓ cup pine nuts
500g/1¼lb young spinach,
stalks removed
2 garlic cloves, crushed
salt and ground black pepper

SERVES 4

1 Put the raisins in a small bowl with boiling water and leave to soak for 10 minutes. Drain.

2 Cut the bread into cubes and discard the crusts. Heat 30ml/ 2 tbsp of the oil and fry the bread until golden. Drain.

3 Heat the remaining oil in the pan. Fry the pine nuts until beginning to colour. Add the spinach and garlic and cook quickly, turning the spinach until it has just wilted.

4 Toss in the raisins and season lightly with salt and pepper. Transfer to a warmed serving dish. Scatter with croûtons and serve hot.

VARIATION
Use Swiss chard or spinach beet instead of the spinach, cooking them a little longer.

SPICED TURNIPS WITH SPINACH AND TOMATOES

Sweet baby turnips, tender spinach and ripe tomatoes make tempting partners in this simple Eastern Mediterranean vegetable stew.

450g/1lb plum or other
well-flavoured tomatoes
60ml/4 tbsp olive oil
2 onions, sliced
450g/1lb baby turnips, peeled
5ml/1 tsp paprika
2.5ml/½ tsp caster sugar
60ml/4 tbsp chopped fresh coriander
450g/1lb fresh young spinach,
stalks removed
salt and ground black pepper

SERVES 6

1 Plunge the tomatoes into a bowl of boiling water for 30 seconds, then refresh in a bowl of cold water. Peel away the tomato skins and chop roughly. Heat the olive oil in a large frying pan or sauté pan and fry the onion slices for about 5 minutes until golden.

2 Add the baby turnips, tomatoes and paprika to the pan with 60ml/4 tbsp water and cook until the tomatoes are pulpy. Cover with a lid and continue cooking until the baby turnips have softened.

3 Stir in the sugar and coriander, then add the spinach and a little salt and pepper and cook for a further 2–3 minutes until the spinach has wilted. Serve warm or cold.

MUSHROOM AND PESTO PIZZA

Home-made Italian-style pizzas are a little time-consuming to make but the results are well worth the effort.

FOR THE PIZZA BASE
350g/12oz/3 cups strong plain flour
1.5ml/¼ tsp salt
15g/½oz easy-blend dried yeast
15ml/1 tbsp olive oil

FOR THE FILLING
50g/2oz dried porcini mushrooms
25g/1oz/¾ cup fresh basil
25g/1oz/⅓ cup pine nuts
40g/1½oz Parmesan cheese, thinly sliced
105ml/7 tbsp olive oil
2 onions, thinly sliced
225g/8oz chestnut mushrooms, sliced
salt and ground black pepper

SERVES 4

1 To make the pizza base, put the flour in a bowl with the salt, dried yeast and olive oil. Add 250ml/ 8fl oz/1 cup hand-hot water and mix to a dough using a round-bladed knife.

2 Turn on to a work surface and knead for 5 minutes until smooth. Place in a clean bowl, cover with clear film and leave in a warm place until doubled in bulk.

3 Meanwhile, make the filling. Soak the dried mushrooms in hot water for 20 minutes. Place the basil, pine nuts, Parmesan and 75ml/5 tbsp of the olive oil in a blender or food processor and process to make a smooth paste. Set the paste aside.

4 Fry the onions in the remaining olive oil for 3–4 minutes until beginning to colour. Add the chestnut mushrooms and fry for 2 minutes. Stir in the drained porcini mushrooms and season lightly.

5 Preheat the oven to 220°C/ 425°F/Gas 7. Lightly grease a large baking sheet. Turn the pizza dough on to a floured surface and roll out to a 30cm/12in round. Place on the baking sheet.

6 Spread the pesto mixture to within 1cm/½in of the edges. Spread the mushroom mixture on top.

7 Bake the pizza for 35–40 minutes until risen and golden.

PAPPARDELLE WITH OLIVE AND CAPER PASTE

This home-made pasta is flavoured with sun-dried tomato paste. The results are well worth the effort, but bought pasta can be substituted for a really quick supper dish.

FOR THE PASTA
275g/10oz/2½ cups plain white flour
1.5ml/¼ tsp salt
3 size 2 eggs
45ml/3 tbsp sun-dried tomato paste

FOR THE SAUCE
115g/4oz/⅔ cup pitted black olives
75ml/5 tbsp capers
5 drained anchovy fillets
1 red chilli, seeded and roughly chopped
60ml/4 tbsp roughly chopped basil
60ml/4 tbsp roughly chopped parsley
150ml/¼ pint/⅔ cup olive oil
4 ripe tomatoes
salt and ground black pepper
flat leaf parsley or basil, to garnish
Parmesan cheese shavings, to serve

SERVES 4

 1 To make the pasta, sift the flour and salt into a bowl and make a well in the centre. Lightly beat the eggs with the tomato paste and pour the mixture into the well.

2 Mix the ingredients together using a round-bladed knife. Turn out on to a work surface and knead for 6–8 minutes until the dough is very smooth and soft, working in a little more flour if it becomes sticky. Wrap in aluminium foil and chill for 30 minutes.

3 To make the sauce, put the olives, capers, anchovies, chilli, basil and parsley in a food processor or blender with the oil. Process very briefly until the ingredients are finely chopped. (Alternatively, you can finely chop the ingredients and then mix with the olive oil.)

4 Plunge the tomatoes into boiling water for 30 seconds, then refresh in cold water. Peel away the skins, remove the seeds and dice. Roll out the dough very thinly on a floured surface. Sprinkle with a little flour, then roll up like a Swiss roll. Cut across into 1cm/½ in slices.

5 Unroll the pasta and lay out on a clean dish towel for about 10 minutes to dry out.

6 Bring a large saucepan of salted water to the boil. Add the pasta and cook for 2–3 minutes until just tender. Drain immediately and return to the saucepan.

7 Add the olive mixture, tomatoes and salt and black pepper to taste, then toss together gently over a moderate heat for about 1 minute until heated through. Garnish with parsley or basil and serve scattered with Parmesan shavings.

BAKED CHEESE POLENTA WITH TOMATO SAUCE

Polenta, or cornmeal, is a staple food in Italy. It is cooked like a sort of porridge, and eaten soft, or set, cut into shapes then baked or grilled.

5ml/1 tsp salt
250g/9oz/2¼ cups quick-cook polenta
5ml/1 tsp paprika
2.5ml/½ tsp ground nutmeg
30ml/2 tbsp olive oil
1 large onion, finely chopped
2 garlic cloves, crushed
2 x 400g/14oz cans chopped tomatoes
15ml/1 tbsp tomato purée
5ml/1 tsp sugar
salt and ground black pepper
75g/3oz Gruyère cheese, grated

SERVES 4

1 Preheat the oven to 200°C/ 400°F/Gas 6. Line a baking tin (28 x 18cm/11 x 7in) with clear film. Bring 1 litre/1¾ pints/4 cups water to the boil with the salt.

2 Pour in the polenta in a steady stream and cook, stirring continuously, for 5 minutes. Beat in the paprika and nutmeg, then pour into the prepared tin and smooth the surface. Leave to cool.

3 Heat the oil in a pan and cook the onion and garlic until soft. Add the tomatoes, purée and sugar. Season. Simmer for 20 minutes.

4 Turn out the polenta on to a chopping board, and cut into 5cm/2in squares. Place half the squares in a greased ovenproof dish. Spoon over half the tomato sauce, and sprinkle with half the cheese. Repeat the layers. Bake for about 25 minutes, until golden.

SPICY CHICK-PEA AND AUBERGINE STEW

This is a Lebanese dish, but similar recipes are found all over the Mediterranean.

3 large aubergines, cubed
200g/7oz/1 cup chick-peas, soaked
overnight
60ml/4 tbsp olive oil
3 garlic cloves, chopped
2 large onions, chopped
2.5ml/½ tsp ground cumin
2.5ml/½ tsp ground cinnamon
2.5ml/½ tsp ground coriander
3 x 400g/14oz cans chopped tomatoes
salt and ground black pepper
cooked rice, to serve

FOR THE GARNISH
30ml/2 tbsp olive oil
1 onion, sliced
1 garlic clove, sliced
sprigs of coriander

SERVES 4

1 Place the aubergines in a colander and sprinkle them with salt. Sit the colander in a bowl and leave for 30 minutes, to allow the bitter juices to escape. Rinse with cold water and dry on kitchen paper.

2 Drain the chick-peas and put in a pan with enough water to cover. Bring to the boil and simmer for 30 minutes, or until tender. Drain.

3 Heat the oil in a large pan. Add the garlic and onion and cook gently, until soft. Add the spices and cook, stirring, for a few seconds. Add the aubergine and stir to coat with the spices and onion. Cook for 5 minutes. Add the tomatoes and chick-peas and season with salt and pepper. Cover and simmer for 20 minutes.

4 To make the garnish, heat the oil in a frying pan and, when very hot, add the sliced onion and garlic. Fry until golden and crisp. Serve the stew with rice, topped with the onion and garlic and garnished with coriander.

SALADS

Summer and salads are synonymous, and nowhere is there a wider variety of these flavoursome dishes than in the Mediterranean. Salads today range from traditional dishes to new creations: the inspiration for salads is endless. Fruit, such as oranges or grapes, make refreshing additions.

ROASTED PEPPERS WITH TOMATOES AND ANCHOVIES

This is a Sicilian-style salad, using some typical ingredients from the Italian island. The flavour
improves if the salad is made and dressed an hour or two before serving.

1 red pepper
1 yellow pepper
4 sun-dried tomatoes in oil, drained
4 ripe plum tomatoes, sliced
2 canned anchovies, drained
and chopped
·15ml/1 tbsp capers, drained
15ml/1 tbsp pine nuts
1 garlic clove, very thinly sliced

FOR THE DRESSING
75ml/5 tbsp extra virgin olive oil
15ml/1 tbsp balsamic vinegar
5ml/1 tsp lemon juice
chopped fresh mixed herbs
salt and ground black pepper

SERVES 4

[1] Cut the peppers in half, and remove the seeds and stalks. Cut into quarters and cook, skin side up, under a hot grill until the skin chars. Transfer to a bowl, and cover with a plate. Leave to cool. Peel the peppers and cut into strips.

[2] Thinly slice the sun-dried tomatoes. Arrange the peppers and fresh tomatoes on a serving dish. Scatter over the anchovies, sun-dried tomatoes, capers, pine nuts and garlic.

[3] To make the dressing, mix together the olive oil, vinegar, lemon juice and chopped herbs and season with salt and pepper. Pour over the salad just before serving.

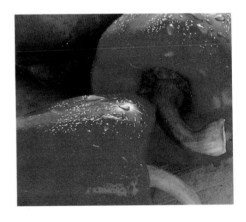

MOROCCAN DATE, ORANGE AND CARROT SALAD

A colourful and unusual salad with exotic ingredients — fresh dates and orange flower water — combined with crisp leaves, carrots, oranges and toasted almonds.

1 Little Gem lettuce
2 carrots, finely grated
2 oranges
115g/4oz fresh dates, stoned and cut into eighths, lengthways
25g/1oz/¼ cup toasted whole almonds, chopped
30ml/2 tbsp lemon juice
5ml/1 tsp caster sugar
1.5ml/¼ tsp salt
15ml/1 tbsp orange flower water

SERVES 4

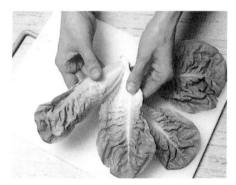

1 Separate the lettuce leaves and arrange them in the bottom of a salad bowl or on individual serving plates. Place the grated carrot in a mound on top.

2 Peel and segment the oranges and arrange them around the carrot. Pile the dates on top, then sprinkle with the almonds. Mix together the lemon juice, sugar, salt and orange flower water and sprinkle over the salad. Serve chilled.

PANZANELLA

In this lively Italian speciality, a sweet tangy blend of tomato juice, rich olive oil and red wine vinegar is soaked up in a colourful salad of roasted peppers, anchovies and toasted ciabatta.

225g/8oz ciabatta (about ⅔ loaf)
150ml/¼ pint/⅔ cup olive oil
3 red peppers
3 yellow peppers
675g/1½lb ripe plum tomatoes
4 garlic cloves, crushed
60ml/4 tbsp red wine vinegar
50g/2oz can anchovy fillets
50g/2oz capers
115g/4oz/1 cup pitted black olives
salt and ground black pepper
basil leaves, to garnish

SERVES 4–6

1 Preheat the oven to 200°C/ 400°F/Gas 6. Cut the ciabatta into 2cm/¾in chunks and drizzle with 50ml/2fl oz/¼ cup of the oil. Grill lightly until just golden.

2 Put the peppers on a foil-lined baking sheet and bake for about 45 minutes until the skin begins to char. Remove from the oven, cover with a cloth and leave to cool slightly.

3 Pull the skin off the peppers and cut them into quarters, discarding the stalk ends and seeds. Drain and then roughly chop the anchovies. Set aside.

4 To make the tomato dressing, peel and halve the tomatoes. Scoop the seeds into a sieve set over a bowl. Using the back of a spoon, press the tomato pulp in the sieve to extract as much juice as possible. Discard the pulp and add the remaining oil, the garlic and vinegar to the juices.

5 Layer the toasted bread, peppers, tomatoes, anchovies, capers and olives in a large salad bowl. Season the tomato dressing with salt and pepper and pour it over the salad. Leave to stand for about 30 minutes. Serve garnished with plenty of basil leaves.

RADICCHIO, ARTICHOKE AND WALNUT SALAD

The distinctive, earthy taste of Jerusalem artichokes makes a lovely contrast to the sharp freshness of radicchio and lemon. Serve warm or cold as an accompaniment to grilled steak or barbecued meats.

1 large radicchio or 150g/5oz
radicchio leaves
40g/1½oz/6 tbsp walnut pieces
45ml/3 tbsp walnut oil
500g/1¼lb Jerusalem artichokes
pared rind and juice of 1 lemon
coarse sea salt and ground
black pepper
flat leaf parsley, to garnish (optional)

SERVES 4

1 If using a whole radicchio, cut it into 8–10 wedges. Put the wedges or leaves in a flameproof dish. Scatter over the walnuts, then spoon over the oil and season. Grill for 2–3 minutes.

2 Peel the artichokes and cut up any large ones so the pieces are all roughly the same size. Add the artichokes to a pan of boiling salted water with half the lemon juice and cook for 5–7 minutes until tender. Drain. Preheat the grill to high.

3 Toss the artichokes into the salad with the remaining lemon juice and the pared rind. Season with coarse salt and pepper. Grill until beginning to brown. Serve at once garnished with torn pieces of parsley, if you like.

WARM BROAD BEAN AND FETA SALAD

This recipe is loosely based on a typical medley of fresh-tasting Greek salad ingredients – broad beans, tomatoes and feta cheese. It's lovely warm or cold as a starter or main course accompaniment.

900g/2lb broad beans, shelled, or 350g/12oz shelled frozen beans
60ml/4 tbsp olive oil
175g/6oz plum tomatoes, halved, or quartered if large
4 garlic cloves, crushed
115g/4oz firm feta cheese, cut into chunks
45ml/3 tbsp chopped fresh dill
12 black olives
salt and ground black pepper
chopped fresh dill, to garnish

SERVES 4–6

1 Cook the fresh or frozen broad beans in boiling, salted water until just tender. Drain and set aside.

2 Meanwhile, heat the oil in a heavy-based frying pan and add the tomatoes and garlic. Cook until the tomatoes are beginning to colour.

3 Add the feta to the pan and toss the ingredients together for 1 minute. Mix with the drained beans, dill, olives and salt and pepper. Serve garnished with chopped dill.

HALLOUMI AND GRAPE SALAD

In Eastern Europe, firm salty halloumi cheese is often served fried for breakfast or supper. In this recipe it's tossed with sweet, juicy grapes which really complement its distinctive flavour.

FOR THE DRESSING
60ml/4 tbsp olive oil
15ml/1 tbsp lemon juice
2.5ml/½ tsp caster sugar
salt and ground black pepper
15ml/1 tbsp chopped fresh thyme or dill

FOR THE SALAD
150g/5oz mixed green salad leaves
75g/3oz seedless green grapes
75g/3oz seedless black grapes
250g/9oz halloumi cheese
45ml/3 tbsp olive oil
fresh young thyme leaves or dill, to garnish

SERVES 4

1 To make the dressing, mix together the olive oil, lemon juice and sugar. Season. Stir in the thyme or dill and set aside.

2 Toss together the salad leaves and the green and black grapes, then transfer to a large serving plate.

3 Thinly slice the cheese. Heat the oil in a large frying pan. Add the cheese and fry briefly until turning golden on the underside. Turn the cheese with a fish slice and cook the other side.

4 Arrange the cheese over the salad. Pour over the dressing and garnish with thyme or dill.

SALAD NICOISE

Made with good quality ingredients, this Provençal salad makes a simple yet unbeatable summer lunch or supper dish. Serve with country-style bread and chilled white wine.

FOR THE DRESSING
90ml/6 tbsp extra virgin olive oil
2 garlic cloves, crushed
15ml/1 tbsp white wine vinegar
salt and ground black pepper

FOR THE SALAD
115g/4oz French beans, trimmed
115g/4oz mixed salad leaves
½ small cucumber, thinly sliced
4 ripe tomatoes, quartered
200g/7oz can tuna in oil, drained
50g/2oz can anchovies, drained
4 eggs, hard-boiled
½ bunch radishes, trimmed
50g/2oz/½ cup small black olives
flat leaf parsley, to garnish

SERVES 4

1 To make the dressing, whisk together the oil, garlic and vinegar and season to taste with salt and pepper.

2 Halve the French beans and cook in a saucepan of boiling water for 2 minutes until only just tender, then drain.

3 Mix the salad leaves, cucumber, tomatoes and beans in a large, shallow salad bowl. Flake the tuna. Halve the anchovies lengthways. Shell and quarter the eggs.

4 Scatter the radishes, tuna, anchovies, eggs and olives over the salad. Pour over the dressing and toss together lightly. Serve garnished with parsley.

SPANISH ASPARAGUS AND ORANGE SALAD

Complicated salad dressings are rarely found in Spain — they simply rely on the wonderful flavour of a good quality olive oil.

225g/8oz asparagus, trimmed and cut
into 5cm/2in pieces
2 large oranges
2 well-flavoured tomatoes, cut
into eighths
50g/2oz romaine lettuce leaves,
shredded
30ml/2 tbsp extra virgin olive oil
2.5ml/½ tsp sherry vinegar
salt and ground black pepper

SERVES 4

COOK'S TIP
Cos or Little Gem lettuce can be used
in place of romaine.

1 Cook the asparagus in boiling, salted water for 3–4 minutes, until just tender. Drain and refresh under cold water.

2 Grate the rind from half an orange and reserve. Peel all the oranges and cut into segments. Squeeze out the juice from the membrane and reserve the juice.

3 Put the asparagus, orange segments, tomatoes and lettuce into a salad bowl. Mix together the oil and vinegar and add 15ml/1 tbsp of the reserved orange juice and 5ml/1 tsp of the rind *(left)*. Season with salt and pepper. Just before serving, pour the dressing over the salad and mix gently to coat.

GLOBE ARTICHOKES WITH GREEN BEANS AND AIOLI

Just like the French aïoli, there are many recipes for the Spanish equivalent. This one is exceptionally garlicky, a perfect partner to freshly cooked vegetables.

FOR THE AIOLI
6 large garlic cloves, sliced
10ml/2 tsp white wine vinegar
250ml/8fl oz/1 cup olive oil
salt and ground black pepper

FOR THE SALAD
225g/8oz green beans
3 small globe artichokes
15ml/1 tbsp olive oil
pared rind of 1 lemon
coarse salt for sprinkling
lemon wedges, to garnish

SERVES 4–6

1 To make the aïoli, put the garlic and vinegar in a blender or mini food processor. With the machine switched on, gradually pour in the olive oil until the mixture is thickened and smooth. (Alternatively, crush the garlic to a paste with the vinegar and gradually beat in the oil using a hand whisk.) Season with salt and pepper to taste.

2 To make the salad, cook the beans in boiling water for 1–2 minutes until slightly softened. Drain.

3 Trim the artichoke stalks close to the base. Cook the artichokes in a large pan of salted water for about 30 minutes, or until you can easily pull away a leaf from the base. Drain well.

4 Using a sharp knife, halve the artichokes lengthways and ease out the choke using a teaspoon.

5 Arrange the artichokes and beans on serving plates and drizzle with the oil. Scatter with the lemon rind and season with coarse salt and a little pepper. Spoon the aïoli into the artichoke hearts and serve warm, garnished with lemon wedges. To eat artichokes, pull the leaves from the base one at a time and use to scoop a little of the sauce. It is only the fleshy end of each leaf that is eaten as well as the base or "heart" of the artichoke.

COOK'S TIP
Mediterranean baby artichokes are sometimes available and are perfect for this kind of salad as, unlike the larger ones, they can be eaten whole. Cook them until just tender, then cut in half to serve.
Canned artichoke hearts, thoroughly drained and sliced, can be substituted when fresh ones are not available.

BROAD BEAN, MUSHROOM AND CHORIZO SALAD

Broad beans are used in both their fresh and dried forms in various Mediterranean countries. This Spanish salad could be served as either a first course or lunch dish.

225g/8oz shelled broad beans
175g/6oz chorizo sausage
60ml/4 tbsp extra virgin olive oil
225g/8oz brown cap
mushrooms, sliced
handful of fresh chives
salt and ground black pepper

SERVES 4

1 Cook the broad beans in boiling, salted water for about 7–8 minutes. Drain and refresh under cold water.

2 Remove the skin from the sausage and cut it into small chunks. Heat the oil in a frying pan, add the chorizo and cook for 2–3 minutes. Tip the chorizo and oil into the mushrooms and mix well. Leave to cool. Chop half the chives. If the beans are large, peel away the tough outer skins. Stir the beans and snipped chives into the mushroom mixture, and season to taste. Serve at room temperature, garnished with the remaining chives.

AVOCADO, ORANGE AND ALMOND SALAD

The Mediterranean is not particularly known for its avocados, but the climate is perfect and they are grown in many parts of the region. This salad has a Spanish influence.

2 oranges
2 well-flavoured tomatoes
2 small avocados
60ml/4 tbsp extra virgin olive oil
30ml/2 tbsp lemon juice
15ml/1 tbsp chopped fresh parsley
1 small onion, sliced into rings
salt and ground black pepper
25g/1oz/¼ cup flaked almonds
and 10–12 black olives,
to garnish

SERVES 4

1 Peel the oranges and slice into thick rounds. Plunge the tomatoes into boiling water for 30 seconds, then refresh in cold water. Peel away the skins, cut into quarters, remove the seeds and chop roughly.

2 Cut the avocados in half, remove the stones and carefully peel away the skin. Cut into chunks.

3 Mix together the olive oil, lemon juice and parsley. Season with salt and pepper. Toss the avocados and tomatoes in half of the dressing.

4 Arrange the sliced oranges on a plate and scatter over the onion rings. Drizzle with the rest of the dressing. Spoon the avocados, tomatoes, almonds and olives on top.

FISH AND SEAFOOD

*Mediterranean fishermen reap a rich harvest of fish and
seafood that can be quite unbeatable. Often simply grilled or
fried, or used as the basis of a soup or stew, these dishes need
little embellishment, except perhaps a crisp salad
and a glass or two of light wine!*

BLACK PASTA WITH SQUID SAUCE

*Tagliatelle flavoured with squid ink looks amazing and tastes deliciously of the sea. You'll find it in good
Italian delicatessens.*

105ml/7 tbsp olive oil
2 shallots, chopped
3 garlic cloves, crushed
45ml/3 tbsp chopped fresh parsley
*675g/1½lb cleaned squid, cut
into rings and rinsed*
150ml/¼ pint/⅔ cup dry white wine
400g/14oz can chopped tomatoes
*2.5ml/½ tsp dried chilli flakes
or powder*
450g/1lb squid ink tagliatelle
salt and ground black pepper

SERVES 4

1 Heat the oil in a pan and add
the shallots. Cook until pale
golden, then add the garlic. When the
garlic colours a little, add 30ml/2 tbsp
of the parsley, stir, then add the squid
and stir again. Cook for 3–4 minutes,
then add the wine.

2 Simmer for a few seconds, then
add the tomatoes and chilli
flakes (*right*) and season with salt and
pepper. Cover and simmer gently for
about 1 hour, until the squid is tender.
Add more water if necessary.

3 Cook the pasta in plenty of
boiling, salted water, according
to the instructions on the packet, or
until *al dente*. Drain and return the
tagliatelle to the pan. Add the squid
sauce and mix well. Sprinkle each
serving with the remaining chopped
parsley and serve at once.

SAUTÉED MUSSELS WITH GARLIC AND HERBS

These mussels are served without their shells, in a delicious paprika flavoured sauce.
Eat them with cocktail sticks.

900g/2lb fresh mussels
1 lemon slice
90ml/6 tbsp olive oil
2 shallots, finely chopped
1 garlic clove, finely chopped
15ml/1 tbsp chopped fresh parsley
2.5ml/½ tsp sweet paprika
1.5ml/¼ tsp dried chilli flakes

SERVES 4

1 Scrub the mussels, discarding any damaged ones that do not close when tapped with a knife. Put the mussels in a large pan, with 250ml/8fl oz/1 cup water, and the slice of lemon. Bring to the boil for 3–4 minutes and remove the mussels as they open. Discard any that remain closed. Take the mussels out of the shells and drain on kitchen paper.

2 Heat the oil in a sauté pan, add the mussels, and cook, stirring, for a minute. Remove from the pan. Add the shallots and garlic and cook, covered, over a low heat, for about 5 minutes, until soft. Remove from the heat and stir in the parsley, paprika and chilli. Return to the heat and stir in the mussels with any juices. Cook briefly. Remove from the heat and cover for a minute or two, to let the flavours mingle, before serving.

GRILLED KING PRAWNS WITH ROMESCO SAUCE

This sauce, from the Catalan region of Spain, is served with fish and seafood. Its main ingredients are sweet pepper, tomatoes, garlic and almonds.

24 raw king prawns
30–45ml/2–3 tbsp olive oil
flat leaf parsley, to garnish
lemon wedges, to serve

FOR THE SAUCE
2 well-flavoured tomatoes
60ml/4 tbsp olive oil
1 onion, chopped
4 garlic cloves, chopped
1 canned pimiento, chopped
2.5ml/½ tsp dried chilli flakes
or powder
75ml/5 tbsp fish stock
30ml/2 tbsp white wine
10 blanched almonds
15ml/1 tbsp red wine vinegar
salt

SERVES 4

1 To make the sauce, immerse the tomatoes in boiling water for about 30 seconds, then refresh them under cold water. Peel away the skins and roughly chop the flesh.

2 Heat 30ml/2 tbsp of the oil in a pan, add the onion and 3 of the garlic cloves and cook until soft. Add the pimiento, tomatoes, chilli, fish stock and wine, then cover and simmer for 30 minutes.

3 Toast the almonds under the grill until golden. Transfer to a blender or food processor and grind coarsely. Add the remaining 30ml/ 2 tbsp of oil, the vinegar and the last garlic clove and process until evenly combined. Add the tomato and pimiento sauce and process until smooth. Season with salt.

4 Remove the heads from the prawns leaving them otherwise unshelled and, with a sharp knife, slit each one down the back and remove the dark vein. Rinse and pat dry on kitchen paper. Preheat the grill. Toss the prawns in olive oil, then spread out in the grill pan. Grill for about 2–3 minutes on each side, until pink. Arrange on a serving platter with the lemon wedges, and the sauce in a small bowl. Serve at once, garnished with parsley.

BRODETTO

The different regions of Italy have their own variations of this dish, but all require a good fish stock. Make sure you buy some of the fish whole so you can simply simmer them, remove the cooked flesh and strain the deliciously flavoured juices to make the stock.

900g/2lb mixture of fish fillets or steaks, such as monkfish, cod, haddock, halibut or hake
900g/2lb mixture of conger eel, red or grey mullet, snapper or small white fish
1 onion, halved
1 celery stick, roughly chopped
225g/8oz squid
225g/8oz fresh mussels
675g/1½lb ripe tomatoes
60ml/4 tbsp olive oil
1 large onion, thinly sliced
3 garlic cloves, crushed
5ml/1 tsp saffron strands
150ml/¼ pint/⅔ cup dry white wine
90ml/6 tbsp chopped fresh parsley
salt and ground black pepper
croûtons, to serve

SERVES 4–5

1 Remove any skin and bones from the fish fillets or steaks, cut the fish into large pieces and reserve. Place the bones in a pan with all the remaining fish.

2 Add the halved onion and the celery and just cover with water. Bring almost to the boil, then reduce the heat and simmer gently for about 30 minutes. Lift out the fish and remove the flesh from the bones. Reserve the stock.

3 To prepare the squid, twist the head and tentacles away from the body. Cut the head from the tentacles. Discard the body contents and peel away the mottled skin. Wash the tentacles and bodies and dry on kitchen paper.

COOK'S TIP
To make the croûtons, cut thin slices from a long thin stick of bread and shallow fry in a little butter until golden.

4 Scrub the mussels, discarding any that are damaged or open ones that do not close when tapped.

5 Plunge the tomatoes into boiling water for 30 seconds, then refresh in cold water. Peel away the skins and chop roughly.

6 Heat the oil in a large saucepan or sauté pan. Add the sliced onion and the garlic and fry gently for 3 minutes. Add the squid and the uncooked white fish, which you reserved earlier, and fry quickly on all sides. Drain.

7 Add 475ml/16fl oz/2 cups strained reserved fish stock, the saffron and tomatoes to the pan. Pour in the wine. Bring to the boil, then reduce the heat and simmer for about 5 minutes. Add the mussels, cover, and cook for 3–4 minutes until the mussels have opened. Discard any that remain closed.

8 Season the sauce with salt and pepper and put all the fish in the pan. Cook gently for 5 minutes. Scatter with the parsley and serve with the croûtons.

SARDINE GRATIN

In Sicily and other countries in the Western Mediterranean, sardines are filled with a robust stuffing, flavoursome enough to compete with the rich oiliness of the fish itself.

15ml/1 tbsp light olive oil
½ small onion, finely chopped
2 garlic cloves, crushed
40g/1½oz/6 tbsp blanched
almonds, chopped
25g/1oz/2 tbsp sultanas,
roughly chopped
10 pitted black olives
30ml/2 tbsp capers, roughly chopped
30ml/2 tbsp roughly chopped
fresh parsley
50g/2oz/1 cup breadcrumbs
16 large sardines, scaled and gutted
25g/1oz/⅓ cup grated
Parmesan cheese
salt and ground black pepper
flat leaf parsley, to garnish

SERVES 4

1. Preheat the oven to 200°C/400°F/Gas 6. Lightly oil a large shallow ovenproof dish.

2. Heat the oil in a frying pan and fry the onion and garlic gently for 3 minutes. Stir in the almonds, sultanas, olives, capers, parsley and 25g/1oz/¼ cup of the breadcrumbs. Season lightly with salt and pepper.

ABOVE: Brodetto (top) and Sardine Gratin (bottom).

3. Make 2–3 diagonal cuts on each side of the sardines. Pack the stuffing into the cavities and lay the sardines in the prepared dish.

4. Mix the remaining breadcrumbs with the cheese and scatter over the fish. Bake for about 20 minutes until the fish is cooked through. Test by piercing one sardine through the thickest part with a knife. Garnish with parsley and serve immediately with a leafy salad.

HAKE AND CLAMS WITH SALSA VERDE

Hake is one of the most popular fish in Spain and here it is cooked in a sauce flavoured with parsley, lemon juice and garlic.

4 hake steaks, about 2cm/³⁄₄in thick
50g/2oz/½ cup plain flour for dusting,
plus 30ml/2 tbsp
60ml/4 tbsp olive oil
15ml/1 tbsp lemon juice
1 small onion, finely chopped
4 garlic cloves, crushed
150ml/¼ pint/²⁄₃ cup fish stock
150ml/¼ pint/²⁄₃ cup white wine
90ml/6 tbsp chopped fresh parsley
75g/3oz frozen petits pois
16 fresh clams
salt and ground black pepper

SERVES 4

1. Preheat the oven to 180°C/ 350°F/Gas 4. Season the fish with salt and pepper, then dust both sides with flour. Heat 30ml/2 tbsp of the oil in a large sauté pan, add the fish and fry for about 1 minute on each side. Transfer to an ovenproof dish and sprinkle with lemon juice.

2. Clean the pan, then heat the remaining oil. Add the onion and garlic and cook until soft. Stir in 30ml/2 tbsp flour and cook for about 1 minute. Gradually add the stock and wine, stirring until thickened and smooth. Add 75ml/5 tbsp of the parsley and the petits pois and season with salt and pepper.

3. Pour the sauce over the fish, and bake in the oven for 15–20 minutes, adding the clams to the dish 3–4 minutes before the end of the cooking time. Discard any clams that do not open, then sprinkle with the remaining parsley before serving.

SICILIAN SPAGHETTI WITH SARDINES

A traditional dish from Sicily, with ingredients that are common to many parts of the Mediterranean.

12 fresh sardines, cleaned and boned
250ml/8fl oz/1 cup olive oil
1 onion, chopped
25g/1oz/¼ cup dill sprigs
50g/2oz/½ cup pine nuts
25g/1oz/2 tbsp raisins, soaked
in water
50g/2oz/½ cup fresh breadcrumbs
450g/1lb spaghetti
flour for dusting
salt

SERVES 4

1 Wash the sardines and pat dry on kitchen paper. Open them out flat, then cut in half lengthways.

2 Heat 30ml/2 tbsp of the oil in a pan, add the onion and fry until golden. Add the dill and cook gently for a minute or two. Add the pine nuts and raisins and season with salt. Dry-fry the breadcrumbs in a frying pan until golden. Set aside.

3 Cook the spaghetti in boiling, salted water according to the instructions on the packet, until *al dente*. Heat the remaining oil in a pan. Dust the sardines with flour and fry in the hot oil for 2–3 minutes. Drain on kitchen paper.

4 Drain the spaghetti and return to the pan. Add the onion mixture and toss well. Transfer the spaghetti mixture to a serving platter and arrange the fried sardines on top. Sprinkle with the toasted breadcrumbs and serve immediately.

SEAFOOD RISOTTO

Risotto is one of Italy's most popular rice dishes and it is made with everything from pumpkin to squid ink. On the Mediterranean shores, seafood is the most obvious addition.

60ml/4 tbsp sunflower oil
1 onion, chopped
2 garlic cloves, crushed
225g/8oz/generous 1 cup arborio rice
105ml/7 tbsp white wine
1.5 litres/2½ pints/6¼ cups hot
fish stock
350g/12oz mixed seafood, such as
raw prawns, mussels, squid rings
or clams
grated rind of ½ lemon
30ml/2 tbsp tomato purée
15ml/1 tbsp chopped fresh parsley
salt and ground black pepper

SERVES 4

1 Heat the oil in a heavy-based pan, add the onion and garlic and cook until soft. Add the rice and stir to coat the grains with oil. Add the wine and cook over a moderate heat, stirring, for a few minutes until absorbed.

2 Add 150ml/¼ pint/⅔ cup of the hot stock and cook, stirring constantly, until the liquid is absorbed by the rice. Continue stirring and adding stock in 150ml/¼ pint/⅔ cup quantities, until half is left. This should take about 10 minutes.

3 Stir in the seafood and cook for 2–3 minutes. Add the remaining stock as before, until the rice is cooked. It should be quite creamy and the grains *al dente*.

4 Stir in the lemon rind, tomato purée and parsley. Season with salt and pepper and serve warm.

ITALIAN PRAWN SKEWERS

Simple and delicious mouthfuls from the Amalfi Coast.

900g/2lb raw tiger prawns, peeled
60ml/4 tbsp olive oil
45ml/3 tbsp vegetable oil
75g/3oz/1¼ cups very fine dry
breadcrumbs
1 garlic clove, crushed
15ml/1 tbsp chopped fresh parsley
salt and ground black pepper
lemon wedges, to serve

SERVES 4

1 Slit the prawns down their backs and remove the dark vein. Rinse in cold water and pat dry.

2 Put the olive oil and vegetable oil in a large bowl and add the prawns, mixing them to coat evenly. Add the breadcrumbs, garlic and parsley and season with salt and pepper. Toss the prawns thoroughly, to give them an even coating of breadcrumbs. Cover and leave to marinate for 1 hour.

3 Thread the prawns on to four metal or wooden skewers, curling them up as you do so, so that the tail is skewered in the middle.

4 Preheat the grill. Place the skewers in the grill pan and cook for about 2 minutes on each side, until the breadcrumbs are golden. Serve with lemon wedges.

ZARZUELA

Zarzuela means "light opera" or "musical comedy" in Spanish and the classic fish stew of the same name should be as lively and colourful as the zarzuela itself. This feast of fish includes lobster and other shellfish, but you can modify the ingredients to suit the occasion and availability.

1 cooked lobster
24 fresh mussels or clams
1 large monkfish tail
225g/8oz squid rings
15ml/1 tbsp plain flour
90ml/6 tbsp olive oil
12 large raw prawns
450g/1lb ripe tomatoes
2 large mild onions, chopped
4 garlic cloves, crushed
30ml/2 tbsp brandy
2 bay leaves
5ml/1 tsp paprika
1 red chilli, seeded and chopped
300ml/½ pint/1¼ cups fish stock
15g/½oz/2 tbsp ground almonds
30ml/2 tbsp chopped fresh parsley
salt and ground black pepper

SERVES 6

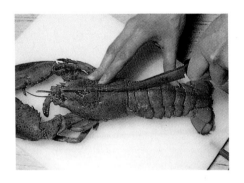

1 Using a large knife, cut the lobster in half lengthways. Remove the dark intestine that runs down the length of the tail. Crack the claws using a hammer.

2 Scrub the mussels, discarding any that are damaged or open ones that do not close when tapped with a knife. Cut the monkfish fillets away from the central cartilage and cut each fillet into three.

3 Toss the monkfish and squid in seasoned flour. Heat the oil in a large frying pan. Add the monkfish and squid and fry quickly; remove from the pan. Fry the prawns on both sides, then remove from the pan.

4 Plunge the tomatoes into boiling water for 30 seconds, then refresh in cold water. Peel away the skins and chop roughly.

5 Add the onions and two-thirds of the garlic to the frying pan and fry for 3 minutes. Add the brandy and ignite with a taper. When the flames die down, add the tomatoes, bay leaves, paprika, chilli and stock.

6 Bring to the boil, reduce the heat and simmer gently for 5 minutes. Add the mussels or clams, cover and cook for 3–4 minutes, until the shells have opened.

7 Remove the mussels or clams from the sauce and discard any that remain closed.

8 Arrange all the fish, including the lobster, in a large flameproof serving dish. Blend the ground almonds to a paste with the remaining garlic and parsley and stir into the sauce. Season with salt and pepper.

9 Pour the sauce over the fish and lobster and cook gently for about 5 minutes until hot. Serve immediately with a green salad and plenty of warmed bread.

MEAT AND POULTRY

The Mediterranean style of cooking makes the most of young lamb and pork, while lighter meats, such as poultry and game, play key roles in regional cuisines right across the Mediterranean. The addition of fruit or vegetables creates sensational flavour combinations.

LAMB WITH RED PEPPERS AND RIOJA

Plenty of garlic, peppers, herbs and red wine give this lamb stew a lovely rich flavour. Slice through the pepper stalks, rather than removing them, as this makes it look extra special.

900g/2lb lean lamb fillet
15ml/1 tbsp plain flour
60ml/4 tbsp olive oil
2 red onions, sliced
4 garlic cloves, sliced
10ml/2 tsp paprika
1.5ml/¼ tsp ground cloves
400ml/14fl oz/1⅔ cups red Rioja
150ml/¼ pint/⅔ cup lamb stock
2 bay leaves
2 thyme sprigs
3 red peppers, halved and seeded
salt and ground black pepper
bay leaves and thyme sprigs,
to garnish
green beans and saffron rice or boiled
potatoes, to serve

SERVES 4

1 Preheat the oven to 160°C/ 325°F/Gas 3. Cut the lamb into chunks. Season the flour, add the lamb and toss lightly to coat.

2 Heat the oil in a frying pan and fry the lamb, stirring, until browned. Transfer to an ovenproof dish. Lightly fry the onions in the pan with the garlic, paprika and cloves.

VARIATION
Use any lean cubed pork instead of the lamb and a white Rioja instead of the red. A mixture of red, yellow and orange peppers looks very effective.

3 Add the Rioja, stock, bay leaves and thyme and bring to the boil, stirring. Pour the contents of the pan over the meat. Cover with a lid and bake for 30 minutes.

4 Remove the dish from the oven. Stir the red peppers into the stew and season lightly with salt and pepper. Bake for a further 30 minutes until the meat is tender. Garnish the stew with bay leaves and sprigs of thyme and serve with green beans and saffron rice or boiled potatoes.

PORK WITH MARSALA AND JUNIPER

Although most frequently used in desserts, Sicilian marsala gives savoury dishes a rich, fruity and alcoholic tang. Use good quality butcher's pork which won't be drowned by the flavour of the sauce.

25g/1oz dried cep or porcini
mushrooms
4 pork escalopes
10ml/2 tsp balsamic vinegar
8 garlic cloves
15g/½oz/1 tbsp butter
45ml/3 tbsp marsala
several rosemary sprigs
10 juniper berries, crushed
salt and ground black pepper
noodles and green vegetables,
to serve

SERVES 4

1 Put the dried mushrooms in a bowl and just cover with hot water. Leave to stand.

2 Brush the pork with 5ml/1 tsp of the vinegar and season with salt and pepper. Put the garlic cloves in a small pan of boiling water and cook for 10 minutes until soft. Drain and set aside.

3 Melt the butter in a large frying pan. Add the pork and fry quickly until browned on the underside. Turn the meat over and cook for another minute.

4 Add the marsala, rosemary, mushrooms, 60ml/4 tbsp of the mushroom juices, the garlic cloves, juniper and remaining vinegar.

5 Simmer gently for about 3 minutes until the pork is cooked through. Season lightly and serve hot with noodles and green vegetables.

CHICKEN THIGHS WITH LEMON AND GARLIC

This recipe uses classic flavourings for chicken. Versions of it can be found in Spain and Italy.
This particular recipe, however, is of French origin.

600ml/1 pint/2½ cups chicken stock
20 large garlic cloves
25g/1oz/2 tbsp butter
15ml/1 tbsp olive oil
8 chicken thighs
1 lemon, peeled, pith removed and
sliced thinly
30ml/2 tbsp plain flour
150ml/¼ pint/⅔ cup dry white wine
salt and ground black pepper
chopped fresh parsley or basil,
to garnish
new potatoes or rice, to serve

SERVES 4

1 Put the stock into a pan and bring to the boil. Add the garlic cloves, cover and simmer gently for 40 minutes. Heat the butter and oil in a sauté or frying pan, add the chicken thighs and cook gently on all sides until golden. Transfer them to an ovenproof dish. Preheat the oven to 190°C/375°F/Gas 5.

2 Strain the stock and reserve it. Distribute the garlic and lemon slices among the chicken pieces. Add the flour to the fat in the pan in which the chicken was browned, and cook, stirring, for 1 minute. Add the wine, stirring constantly and scraping the bottom of the pan, then add the stock. Cook, stirring, until the sauce has thickened and is smooth. Season with salt and pepper.

3 Pour the sauce over the chicken, cover, and cook in the oven for 40–45 minutes. If a thicker sauce is required, lift out the chicken pieces, and reduce the sauce by boiling rapidly, until it reaches the desired consistency. Scatter over the chopped parsley or basil and serve with boiled new potatoes or rice.

POLPETTES WITH MOZZARELLA AND TOMATO

These Italian meatballs are made with beef and topped with mozzarella cheese and tomato.

½ slice white bread, crusts removed
45ml/3 tbsp milk
675g/1½lb minced beef
1 egg, beaten
50g/2oz/⅔ cup dry breadcrumbs
vegetable oil for frying
2 beefsteak or other large
tomatoes, sliced
15ml/1 tbsp chopped fresh oregano
1 mozzarella cheese, cut into 6 slices
6 drained canned anchovies, cut in
half lengthways
salt and ground black pepper

SERVES 6

1 Preheat the oven to 200°C/ 400°F/Gas 6. Put the bread and milk into a small saucepan and heat very gently, until the bread absorbs all the milk. Mash it to a pulp and leave to cool.

2 Put the beef into a bowl with the bread mixture and the egg and season with salt and pepper. Mix well, then shape the mixture into six patties. Sprinkle the breadcrumbs on to a plate and dredge the patties, coating them thoroughly.

3 Heat about 5mm/¼in oil in a large frying pan. Add the patties and fry for 2 minutes on each side, until brown. Transfer to a greased ovenproof dish, in a single layer.

4 Lay a slice of tomato on top of each patty, sprinkle with oregano and season with salt and pepper. Place the mozzarella slices on top. Arrange two strips of anchovy, placed in a cross on top of each slice of mozzarella.

5 Bake for 10–15 minutes, until the mozzarella has melted. Serve hot, straight from the dish.

OLIVE OIL ROASTED CHICKEN WITH MEDITERRANEAN VEGETABLES

This is a delicious French alternative to a traditional roast chicken. Use a corn-fed or free-range bird, if available. This recipe also works well with guinea fowl.

1.75kg/4–4½lb roasting chicken
150ml/¼ pint/⅔ cup extra virgin
olive oil
½ lemon
few sprigs of fresh thyme
450g/1lb small new potatoes
1 aubergine, cut into 2.5cm/1in cubes
1 red pepper, seeded and quartered
1 fennel bulb, trimmed and quartered
8 large garlic cloves, unpeeled
coarse salt and ground black pepper

SERVES 4

2 Remove the chicken from the oven and season with salt. Turn the chicken right side up, and baste with the juices from the pan. Surround the bird with the potatoes, roll them in the pan juices, and return the roasting pan to the oven, to continue roasting.

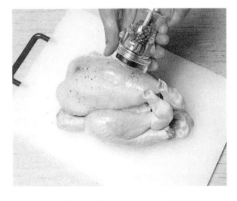

1 Preheat the oven to 200°C/400°F/Gas 6. Rub the chicken all over with olive oil and season with pepper. Place the lemon half inside the bird, with a sprig or two of thyme. Put the chicken breast side down in a large roasting pan. Roast for about 30 minutes.

3 After 30 minutes, add the aubergine, red pepper, fennel and garlic cloves to the pan. Drizzle with the remaining oil, and season with salt and pepper. Add any remaining thyme to the vegetables. Return to the oven, and cook for 30–50 minutes more, basting and turning the vegetables occasionally.

4 To find out if the chicken is cooked, push the tip of a sharp knife between the thigh and breast. If the juices run clear, it is done. The vegetables should be tender and just beginning to brown. Serve the chicken and vegetables from the pan, or transfer the vegetables to a serving dish, joint the chicken and place it on top. Serve the skimmed juices in a gravy boat.

PIGEON BREASTS WITH PANCETTA

Mild succulent pigeon breasts are easy to cook and make an impressive main course for a special dinner.
Serve this Italian-style dish with polenta and some simple green vegetables.

4 whole pigeons
2 large onions
2 carrots, roughly chopped
1 celery stick, trimmed and
roughly chopped
25g/1oz dried porcini mushrooms
50g/2oz pancetta
25g/1oz/2 tbsp butter
30ml/2 tbsp olive oil
2 garlic cloves, crushed
150ml/¼ pint/⅔ cup red wine
salt and ground black pepper
flat leaf parsley, to garnish
cooked oyster mushrooms, to serve

SERVES 4

2 Put the pigeon carcasses in a large saucepan. Halve one of the onions, leaving the skin on. Add to the pan with the carrots and celery and just cover with water. Bring to the boil, reduce the heat and simmer very gently, uncovered, for about 1½ hours to make a dark, rich stock. Leave to cool slightly, then strain through a large sieve into a bowl.

3 Cover the dried mushrooms with 150ml/¼ pint/⅔ cup hot water and soak for 30 minutes. Cut the pancetta into small dice.

1 To prepare a pigeon, cut down the length of the bird, just to one side of the breastbone. Gradually scrape away the meat from the breastbone until the breast comes away completely. Do the same on the other side then repeat with the remaining pigeons.

4 Peel and finely chop the remaining onion. Melt half the butter with the oil in a large frying pan. Add the onion and pancetta and fry very gently for 3 minutes. Add the pigeon breasts, skin sides down and fry for 2 minutes until browned. Turn over and fry for a further 2 minutes.

5 Add the mushrooms, with the soaking liquid, garlic, wine and 250ml/8fl oz/1 cup of the stock. Bring just to the boil, then reduce the heat and simmer gently for 5 minutes until the pigeon breasts are tender, but still a little pink in the centre.

6 Lift out the pigeon breasts and keep them hot. Return the sauce to the boil and boil rapidly to reduce slightly. Gradually whisk in all the remaining butter and season with salt and pepper to taste.

7 Transfer the pigeon breasts to warmed serving plates and pour over the sauce. Serve at once, garnished with sprigs of parsley and accompanied by oyster mushrooms.

COOK'S TIP
If buying pigeons from a butcher, order them in advance and ask him to remove the breasts for you. You can also joint the legs and fry these with the breasts, although there is little meat on them and you might prefer to let them flavour the stock.

BREADS, PASTRIES AND DESSERTS

Bread, a staple food all over the Mediterranean, comes in a remarkable variety of flavours and textures, while sumptuous pastries and desserts provide a fabulous finale to any meal.

SUN-DRIED TOMATO BREAD

In the south of Italy, tomatoes are often dried off in the hot sun. They are then preserved in oil, or hung up in strings in the kitchen, to use in the winter. This recipe uses the former.

675g/1½lb/6 cups strong plain flour
10ml/2 tsp salt
25g/1oz/2 tbsp caster sugar
25g/1oz fresh yeast
400–475ml/14–16fl oz/1⅔–2 cups warm milk
15ml/1 tbsp tomato purée
75ml/5 tbsp oil from the jar of sun-dried tomatoes
75ml/5 tbsp extra virgin olive oil
75g/3oz/¾ cup drained sun-dried tomatoes, chopped
1 large onion, chopped

MAKES 4 SMALL LOAVES

2 Mix the tomato purée into the remaining milk, until evenly blended, then add to the flour with the tomato oil and olive oil.

3 Gradually mix the flour into the liquid ingredients, until you have a dough. Turn out on to a floured surface, and knead for about 10 minutes, until smooth and elastic. Return to the clean bowl, cover with a cloth, and leave to rise in a warm place for about 2 hours.

4 Knock the dough back, and add the tomatoes and onion. Knead until evenly distributed through the dough. Shape into four rounds and place on a greased baking sheet. Cover with a dish towel and leave to rise again for about 45 minutes.

5 Preheat the oven to 190°C/ 375°F/Gas 5. Bake the bread for 45 minutes, or until the loaves sound hollow when you tap them underneath with your fingers. Leave to cool on a wire rack. Eat warm, or toasted with grated mozzarella cheese on top.

1 Sift the flour, salt and sugar into a bowl, and make a well in the centre. Crumble the yeast, mix with 150ml/¼ pint/⅔ cup of the warm milk and add to the flour.

COOK'S TIP
Use a pair of sharp kitchen scissors to cut up the sun-dried tomatoes.

OLIVE BREAD

Olive breads are popular all over the Mediterranean. For this Greek recipe use rich oily olives or those marinated in herbs rather than canned ones.

2 red onions, thinly sliced
30ml/2 tbsp olive oil
225g/8oz/1⅓ cups pitted black or
green olives
750g/1¾lb/7 cups strong plain flour
7.5ml/1½ tsp salt
20ml/4 tsp easy-blend dried yeast
45ml/3 tbsp each roughly chopped
parsley, coriander or mint

MAKES TWO 675G/1½LB LOAVES

1 Fry the onions in the oil until soft. Roughly chop the olives.

2 Put the flour, salt, yeast and parsley, coriander or mint in a large bowl with the olives and fried onions and pour in 475ml/16fl oz/ 2 cups hand-hot water.

VARIATION
Shape the dough into 16 small rolls. Slash the tops as above and reduce the cooking time to 25 minutes.

3 Mix to a dough using a round-bladed knife, adding a little more water if the mixture feels dry.

4 Turn out on to a lightly floured surface and knead for about 10 minutes. Put in a clean bowl, cover with clear film and leave in a warm place until doubled in bulk.

5 Preheat the oven to 220°C/ 425°F/Gas 7. Lightly grease two baking sheets. Turn the dough on to a floured surface and cut in half. Shape into two rounds and place on the baking sheets. Cover loosely with lightly oiled clear film and leave until doubled in size.

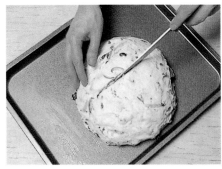

6 Slash the tops of the loaves with a knife then bake for about 40 minutes or until the loaves sound hollow when tapped on the bottom. Transfer to a wire rack to cool.

FOCACCIA

This is a flattish bread, originating from Genoa in Italy, made with flour, olive oil and salt. There are many variations, from many regions, including stuffed varieties, and versions topped with onions, olives or herbs.

25g/1oz fresh yeast
400g/14oz/3½ cups strong plain flour
10ml/2 tsp salt
75ml/5 tbsp olive oil
10ml/2 tsp coarse sea salt

MAKES 1 ROUND 25CM/10IN LOAF

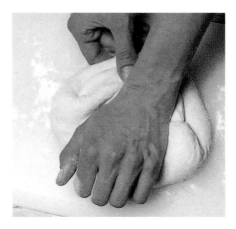

1 Dissolve the yeast in 120ml/ 4fl oz/½ cup warm water. Allow to stand for 10 minutes. Sift the flour into a large bowl, make a well in the centre, and add the yeast, salt and 30ml/2 tbsp oil. Mix in the flour and add more water to make a dough.

2 Turn out on to a floured surface and knead the dough for about 10 minutes, until smooth and elastic. Return to the bowl, cover with a cloth, and leave to rise in a warm place for 2–2½ hours until the dough has doubled in bulk.

3 Knock back the dough and knead again for a few minutes. Press into an oiled 25cm/10in tart tin, and cover with a damp cloth. Leave to rise for 30 minutes.

4 Preheat the oven to 200°C/ 400°F/Gas 6. Poke the dough all over with your fingers, to make little dimples in the surface. Pour the remaining oil over the dough, using a pastry brush to take it to the edges. Sprinkle with the salt.

5 Bake for 20–25 minutes, until the bread is a pale gold. Carefully remove from the tin and leave to cool on a rack. The bread is best eaten on the same day, but it also freezes very well.

FRESH FIGS WITH HONEY AND WINE

Any variety of figs can be used in this recipe, their ripeness determining the cooking time. Choose ones that are plump and firm, and use quickly as they don't store well.

450ml/¾ pint/1⅞ cups dry white wine
75g/3oz/⅓ cup clear honey
50g/2oz/¼ cup caster sugar
1 small orange
8 whole cloves
450g/1lb fresh figs
1 cinnamon stick
mint sprigs, or bay leaves, to decorate

FOR THE CREAM
300ml/½ pint/1¼ cups double cream
1 vanilla pod
5ml/1 tsp caster sugar

SERVES 6

1 Put the wine, honey and sugar in a heavy-based saucepan and heat gently until the sugar dissolves.

2 Stud the orange with the cloves and add to the syrup with the figs and cinnamon. Cover and simmer very gently for 5–10 minutes until the figs are softened. Transfer to a serving dish and leave to cool.

3 Put 150ml/¼ pint/⅔ cup of the cream in a small saucepan with the vanilla pod. Bring almost to the boil, then leave to cool and infuse for 30 minutes. Remove the vanilla pod and mix with the remaining cream and sugar in a bowl. Whip lightly. Transfer to a serving dish. Decorate the figs, then serve with the cream.

ICED ORANGES

These little sorbets served in the fruit shell were originally sold in the beach cafés in the south of France. They are pretty and easy to eat — a good picnic treat to store in the cold box.

150g/5oz/⅔ cup granulated sugar
juice of 1 lemon
14 medium oranges
8 fresh bay leaves, to decorate

SERVES 8

1   Put the sugar in a heavy-based pan. Add half the lemon juice, and 120ml/4fl oz/½ cup water. Cook over a low heat until the sugar has dissolved. Bring to the boil, and boil for 2–3 minutes, until the syrup is clear. Leave to cool.

2   Slice the tops off eight of the oranges, to make "hats". Scoop out the flesh of the oranges, and reserve. Put the empty orange shells and "hats" on a tray and place in the freezer until needed.

3   Grate the rind of the remaining oranges and add to the syrup. Squeeze the juice from the oranges, and from the reserved flesh. There should be 750ml/1¼ pints/3 cups. Squeeze another orange or add bought orange juice, if necessary.

4   Stir the orange juice and remaining lemon juice, with 90ml/6 tbsp water into the syrup. Taste, adding more lemon juice or sugar, as desired. Pour the mixture into a shallow freezer container and freeze for 3 hours.

5   Turn the mixture into a bowl, and whisk to break down the ice crystals. Freeze for 4 hours more, until firm, but not solid.

6   Pack the mixture into the orange shells, mounding it up, and set the "hats" on top. Freeze until ready to serve. Just before serving, push a skewer into the tops of the "hats" and push in a bay leaf.

COOK'S TIP
Use crumpled kitchen paper to keep the shells upright.

WALNUT AND RICOTTA CAKE

Soft, tangy ricotta cheese is widely used in Italian sweets. Here, it is included along with walnuts and orange to flavour a whisked egg sponge. Don't worry if it sinks slightly after baking — this gives it an authentic appearance.

115g/4oz/1 cup walnut pieces
150g/5oz/⅔ cup unsalted butter, softened
150g/5oz/⅔ cup caster sugar
5 eggs, separated
finely grated rind of 1 orange
150g/5oz/⅔ cup ricotta cheese
40g/1½oz/6 tbsp plain flour

To finish
60ml/4 tbsp apricot jam
30ml/2 tbsp brandy
50g/2oz bitter or plain chocolate, coarsely grated

MAKES 10 SLICES

1 Preheat the oven to 190°C/ 375°F/Gas 5. Grease and line the base of a deep 23cm/9in round, loose-based cake tin. Roughly chop and lightly toast the walnuts.

2 Cream together the butter and 115g/4oz/½ cup of the sugar until light and fluffy. Add the egg yolks, orange rind, ricotta cheese, flour and walnuts and mix together.

3 Whisk the egg whites in a large bowl until stiff. Gradually whisk in the remaining sugar. Using a large metal spoon, fold a quarter of the whisked whites into the ricotta mixture. Carefully fold in the rest of the whisked whites.

4 Turn the mixture into the prepared tin and level the surface. Bake for about 30 minutes until risen and firm. Leave the cake to cool in the tin.

5 Transfer the cake to a serving plate. Heat the apricot jam in a small saucepan with 15ml/1 tbsp water. Press through a sieve and stir in the brandy. Use to coat the top and sides of the cake. Scatter the cake generously with grated chocolate.

VARIATION
Use toasted and chopped almonds in place of the walnuts.

BISCOTTI

These lovely Italian biscuits are part-baked, sliced to reveal a feast of mixed nuts and then baked again
until crisp and golden. Traditionally they're served dipped in Vin Santo, a sweet dessert wine - perfect
for rounding off a Mediterranean meal.

50g/2oz/¼ cup unsalted butter,
softened
115g/4oz/½ cup caster sugar
175g/6oz/1½ cups self-raising flour
1.5ml/¼ tsp salt
10ml/2 tsp baking powder
5ml/1 tsp ground coriander
finely grated rind of 1 lemon
50g/2oz/½ cup polenta
1 egg, lightly beaten
10ml/2 tsp brandy or orange-
flavoured liqueur
50g/2oz/½ cup unblanched almonds
50g/2oz/½ cup pistachio nuts

MAKES 24

1 Preheat the oven to 160°C/
325°F/Gas 3. Lightly grease a
baking sheet. Cream together the
butter and sugar.

2 Sift all the flour, salt, baking
powder and coriander into the
bowl. Add the lemon rind, polenta,
egg and brandy or liqueur and mix
together to make a soft dough.

3 Stir in the nuts until evenly
combined. Halve the mixture.
Shape each half into a flat sausage
about 23cm/9in long and 6cm/2½in
wide. Bake for about 30 minutes until
risen and just firm. Remove from oven.

4 When cool, cut each sausage
diagonally into 12 thin slices.
Return to the baking sheet and cook
for a further 10 minutes until crisp.

5 Transfer to a wire rack to cool
completely. Store in an airtight
tin for up to 1 week.

COOK'S TIP
Use a sharp, serrated knife to slice the
cooled biscuits, otherwise they will
crumble.

DATE AND ALMOND TART

Fresh dates make an unusual but delicious filling for a tart. The influences here are French and Middle Eastern — a true Mediterranean fusion!

FOR THE PASTRY
175g/6oz/1½ cups plain flour
75g/3oz/6 tbsp butter
1 egg

FOR THE FILLING
90g/3½oz/scant ½ cup butter
90g/3½oz/7 tbsp caster sugar
1 egg, beaten
*90g/3½oz/scant 1 cup ground
almonds*
30ml/2 tbsp plain flour
30ml/2 tbsp orange flower water
12–13 fresh dates, halved and stoned
60ml/4 tbsp apricot jam

SERVES 6

1 Preheat the oven to 200°C/ 400°F/Gas 6. Place a baking sheet in the oven. Sift the flour into a bowl, add the butter and work with your fingertips until the mixture resembles fine breadcrumbs. Add the egg and a tablespoon of cold water, then work to a smooth dough.

2 Roll out the pastry on a lightly floured surface and use to line a 20cm/8in tart tin. Prick the base with a fork, then chill until needed.

3 To make the filling, cream the butter and sugar until light, then beat in the egg. Stir in the ground almonds, flour and 15ml/1 tbsp of the orange flower water, mixing well.

4 Spread the mixture evenly over the base of the pastry case. Arrange the dates, cut side down, on the almond mixture. Bake on the hot baking sheet for 10–15 minutes, then reduce the heat to 180°C/350°F/Gas 4. Bake for a further 15–20 minutes until light golden and set.

5 Transfer the tart to a rack to cool. Gently heat the apricot jam, then press through a sieve. Add the remaining orange flower water.

6 Brush the tart with the jam and serve at room temperature.

INDEX